PERSPECTIVE

Jan Vredeman de Vries

PERSPECTIVE

WITH A NEW INTRODUCTION

by Adolf K. Placzek

AVERY LIBRARY   *   COLUMBIA UNIVERSITY

Dover Publications, Inc., New York

Published in Canada by General Publishing Company, Ltd.,
30 Lesmill Road, Don Mills, Toronto, Ontario.
Published in the United Kingdom by Constable and Company, Ltd.
10 Orange Street, London WC 2.

This Dover edition, first published in 1968, is a republication of the work originally published by Henricus Hondius in Leiden in 1604 and *(Pars altera)* 1605. The text which accompanied the illustrations has been omitted in this reprint. A new Introduction has been written specially for the present edition by Adolf K. Placzek. The translations appearing on pages viii, x, xii, xiv, and 50 are by Stanley Appelbaum.

Standard Book Number: 486-21086-4
Library of Congress Catalog Card Number: 67-16701

MANUFACTURED IN THE UNITED STATES OF AMERICA
Dover Publications, Inc.
180 Varick Street
New York, N.Y. 10014

INTRODUCTION TO THE DOVER EDITION

Very little is known about Jan (or Hans, as he is often called) Vredeman de Vries, the architect-painter-engraver whose impact and influence throughout Northern Europe was to be so marked. We know that he was born in 1527 in Leeuwaarden, a town in Dutch Friesland. He was trained as a painter, but soon became interested in architecture, at the time when the great Italian Renaissance movement finally reached the Netherlands. For a while he lived in Antwerp, but had to flee from the Duke of Alba's edict in 1570 against heresy and heretics at the height of the Spanish war. He went back to Antwerp a few years later, then worked in Germany as an architect, tried to form a painters' guild in Danzig, later turned up at the famous court of the Emperor Rudolph II in Prague and finally returned to Holland, where he lived with his painter-son Paul. The date of his death is uncertain, probably around 1604, at the time of the publication of this book.

Vredeman's unsettled life is a true reflection of the turbulent time he lived in—particularly turbulent in his native country, which had to fight so long and so hard for its religious freedom and national independence. His work is an equally true reflection of the artistic cross currents of his time: Northern and Southern elements, Gothic, Renaissance, Baroque and Mannerism are all represented in a powerful combination expressive of the Netherlands of the late sixteenth century. And since the Netherlands were in many ways the center of the Northern Renaissance, Vredeman can certainly be considered a principal messenger of the new style throughout Germany, Scandinavia and even the British Isles.

Vredeman worked as an architect, but no building known surely to be his has survived. His paintings—many of architectural vistas—are of historical interest, but not much more. His true and great importance rests on his numerous engravings, in which he opened new avenues of architectural invention and architectural representation. His books are fantasies and textbooks, dreams and pattern-books for apprentices, avant-garde messages and popular pictures—all at the same time. From 1555 to his death the indefatigable master produced publication after publication on architectural topics, the flow of which did not cease even at his death, since restrikes and new editions continued to appear from Amsterdam and Antwerp. His early engravings deal with scrolls, cartouches, grotesques and arabesques. He then turned to the five orders of architecture—as we know, a great preoccupation of his time. His attempt to popularise classic forms in the North, which was slow to accept them, earned him the name of "Flemish Vitruvius." In 1565 his first series on gardens appeared: formal designs which had a most definite influence on landscape architecture. His early attempts in perspective (1568) were not successful (this series has erroneously been taken for the first edition of his later book). His manneristic architectural fantasies appeared under the title *Variae Architecturae Formae* in 1601.

His last and greatest work is his *Perspective* (or, as he calls it in the subtitle, the "most famous art of eyesight"), published in The Hague and in Leiden in 1604–1605 by the great publishing house of Hondius. The book is dedicated to Prince Maurice of Nassau, Stadholder of Holland and Zeeland, head of the newly established independent country, younger son of the famous William the Silent. It consists of two parts, 49 plates in the first (33/34 being a double plate) and 24 in the second, with short comments on each plate, the whole introduced by a preface of only a few words, since, as Vredeman charmingly says, he did not want to be tiresome or tedious to his readers, but would let his illustrations speak for themselves.

The rules of perspective were, of course, by then nothing new. They had been formulated in the fifteenth century in Italy by Piero della Francesca, Leon Battista Alberti and others, had been refined in the sixteenth century by Serlio and Vignola and were thoroughly familiar to Leonardo, Raphael and all the other great Italian painters. In Germany Albrecht Dürer had worked with perspective, and it is Dürer on whom Vredeman, according to his own statement, based much of his knowledge.

The basic principles from which Vredeman proceeds seem quite obvious. They consist in the establishment of vanishing points into which all lines, which in actual fact are parallel to each other, converge. All vanishing points rest on a vanishing line or horizon line (that is, assuming that we are looking straight ahead, not upward or downward). The forward vanishing point, or, as he calls it, the "eye point," need not be in the center, but can be to the right or left of center, depending on the position of the viewer. Vredeman then reiterates the fundamental rule of all perspective. As he puts it: whatever is *above* the horizon cannot be seen from above, and whatever is *below* the horizon cannot be seen from below. He establishes a gridwork of five linear components into which, to achieve an illusion of space, all objects can be placed. These five linear components are:

1. The base line that defines the level on which the imaginary viewer or painter stands.

2. The perpendicular lines that frame the whole system.

3. The horizon line, already mentioned.

4. The parallel lines, or lines of foreshortening, that converge at the "eye point" or central vanishing point.

5. The diagonal or oblique lines that converge at distance points, or secondary vanishing points.

Vredeman also states that, throughout his book, he has assumed the unchanging eye level of a rather small-sized man, five and a half feet high—an assumption not borne out by some of his plates (I-14, I-16), which appear to represent a far higher angle of vision. This man, incidentally, appears in Plate I-30 in person—as both the viewer and viewed.

Vredeman, like most other masters of perspective, also has his viewer look up into interior architectural space, into a dome or a vault (as in Plates I-37 and I-38) or down a many-tiered stairwell (I-39). Exciting views result. Here the rules of perspective are, of course, somewhat differently applied. Only one vanishing point and no horizon line is needed, and this vanishing point has nothing to do with eye level, but depends only on the position of the viewer below or above, and the direction in which he is looking.

The beauty of the plates and the ingenuity and clarity of Vredeman's demonstrations are self-evident. Even to the present-day enquirer they still clearly reveal the elements of perspective. Beyond this, there is also his vivid architectural imagination, as in the Renaissance fantasies of Plates I-46 and II-10, in the lovely Gothic interior of Plate I-47 and in the exquisite medieval townscapes of Plates II-14 and II-15. It is with these designs that Vredeman de Vries will continue to delight those who turn to him, as he has throughout the centuries.

Adolf K. Placzek

Avery Library
Columbia University
1967

Translation of Latin title page (facing page):

PERSPECTIVE

That is, the Most famous art of eyesight, which looks upon or through objects, on a painted wall, panel or canvas; in which are shown certain ancient as well as modern buildings, Temples or Shrines, Palaces, Private Apartments, Porticos, Streets, Promenades, Gardens, Marketplaces, Roads and other such constructions, resting on their fundamental lines, their basis being clearly explained with descriptions; an art of the greatest utility and necessity for all Painters, Engravers, Sculptors, Metalworkers, Architects, Designers, Masons, Cabinetmakers, Carpenters and all lovers of the arts who may wish to apply themselves to this art with greater pleasure and less pain.

By Jan Vredeman de Vries [the Frisian, or Frieslander].

ENGRAVED AND LEGALLY PUBLISHED BY
HENRICUS HONDIUS
LEIDEN

PERSPECTIVE

Id eſt, Celeberrima ars inſpicientis aut tranſpicientis oculorum aciei, in pariete, tabula aut tela depicta, in qua demonſtrantur quædam tam antiqua, quam nova ædificia, Templorum ſive Ædium, Aularum, Cubicularum, Ambulaciorum, Platearum, Xyſtorum, Hortorum, Fororum, Viarum, & hujuſmodi alia, quæ nituntur ſuis fondamentalibus lineis, quorum fondamentum deſcriptionibus clarè exſplicatur, pervtilis ac neceſſaria, omnibus Pictoribus, Sculptoribus, Statuariis, Fabriferrariis, Architectis, Inventoribus, Cæmentariis, Scrinariis, Fabrilignariis, & omnibus artium amatoribus, qui huic arti operam dare volent, majori cum voluptate, & minori cum labore.

Auctore Ioanne Vredeman Friſo.

HENRIC. HONDIVS SCVLPS ET EXCVD CVM PRIVILL.

LVGDVNI   BATAVORVM

Translation of dedication to Maurice (facing page):

[Around and under portrait: Maurice, born by the grace of God Prince of Orange, Count of Nassau, Marquis of Ter Veere and Flushing and Governor (Stadholder) of the United Provinces of Belgium. . . . At length the slip becomes a tree. . . . Engraved and legally published by Henricus Hondius, 1599.]

To the Most Illustrious and Generous
Prince and Lord, the Lord
MAURICE
PRINCE OF ORANGE, COUNT
OF NASSAU, ETC.

Marquis of Ter Veere and Flushing, Governor and Commander-in-Chief
of the Army of the United Provinces of Belgium,
and their Supreme Admiral, etc.

On whom God showers virtues numberless,
Him rightly do good men revere. The health
He craves they cry to heaven for, and bless
Him always with their prayers for weal and wealth.
God and your virtue raised you to this station,
O Prince. All know your virtue; your deep care
For godliness and for our holy nation
Has spread that virtue's power everywhere.
I reverence you. Scientific lore
Is safely garnered while you rule our state,
And arts that suit a Prince. To you, therefore,
My well-wrought Optics do I dedicate.
It won approval in your mind, your sight,
Then from the law. My eyes to you I raise:
Prince, look upon me in a kindly light—
For it is you whose virtue draws each gaze.

Your Excellency's

most devoted bondsman

J. VREDEMAN DE VRIES

Henricus bondius fecit et excudit; Cum priuillegio.
1599

Illuſtriſsimo Generoſiſsimóque
Principi ac Domino, Domino
MAVRITIO,
PRINCIPI AVRIACO, COMITI
à NASSAV, &c.

Marchioni Veriæ & Fliſsingæ; Gubernatori Præfectóque
Militum ſummo Confœderatarum BELGII
Provinciarum, earumdémque
Archithalaſſo, &c.

Quem Deus innumeris animi virtutibus ornat,
Iure boni obſervant, exoptatámque ſalutem
Supplicibus votis atque omnia fauſta precantur.
Te Deus (t) Virtus tua, Princeps, extulit: omni
Nota Viro Virtus: quam Relligionis amore
Et Patriæ ſanctæ parteis diffundis in omnes.
Te colo, te veneror: te Principe dîa Matheſis
Eſt ſalva, atque artes ſunt ſalvæ Principe dignæ.
Hinc Tibi ſeſe offert bene culta hæc Optica noſtra,
Quæ ingenio eſt oculiſque tuis, tum lege probata.
Quo bene proſpicimus auctorem reſpice PRINCEPS:
Es ſiquidem, cujus virtus ſpectatur ab omni.

Excellentiæ Tuæ

devotiſsimus cliens

I. VREDEMAN FRISIVS.

â

Translation of address to the nobility of Frisia [Friesland] (facing page):

To the most Noble and Honorable Men,

THE LORDS

OF THE STATES OF FRISIA:

And also

To the most Famous and Prudent Senators of the City

OF LEEUWAARDEN.

Since I am sprung from famed Leeuwaarden's soil,
And all are moved by love of fatherland:
To you, my Lords, I dedicate this toil,
Who fatherlike our nation do command,
Our land that William, Nassau's hero, sways.
Accept, Leeuwaarden, from a grateful heart
This book that to the realms of light displays—
And amply illustrates—the Optic Art.
Not small the task. The honor which is due
This art be shown it. Frisia, 't was for you
A Frisian wrought this. May your eyes with cheer
Gaze on this *Optics* that I offer here.

Your Honors'

most humble servant

J. VREDEMAN DE VRIES

Nobilißimis Amplißimifque Viris,

D D.

ORDINIBVS FRISIÆ:

Item

Clarißimis Prudentißimifque Senatoribus Urbis

LEOVARDIENSIS.

CVm natale folum mihi fit LEOVARDIA clara,
Omnes & dulcis Patriæ ducantur amore;
Hoc *Patriæ* moveor *Patribus* facrare Labores
Hofce meos, & cui GVILLELMVS præfidet Heros
NASSOVIVS. Noftri tuque ô *Leovardia* teftem
Grati habeas animi Librum hunc, in luminis oras
Optica quo prodit, variis expreffa figuris.
Non labor exiguus. fit honos & debitus arti
Huic aliquis. Scripto hoc ftuduit tibi, *Frifia*, Frifo.
Afpicite hanc oculis, quę fe offert *Optica*, lętis.

Veftræ Amplitud.

humillimus fubditus

I. VREDEMAN FRISO.

Translation of address to the readers (facing page):

[Beneath portrait of Vredeman: Aetat. 77 = "At the age of 77."]

TO THE STUDIOUS VIEWERS
OF OPTICS.

This is my visage. From youth's earliest flower
Revering art, I strove that not one hour
Should idly pass. My eyes and mind took pride
In sacred Optics. *Thereunto allied*
Was fructifying labor; forty years
I plied this art devoutly. Here appears
A doctrine won by toil. That art is famed
For trustiness which trusty rules have framed:
And here most trusty methods shall explain
This art, which guides the eyes and soothes the brain
With images, but never cheats the sight
With lying views. For your more true delight
Exact engravings illustrate this book.
Here I may gain renown . . . Let Belgium look
Toward her own name for learning, if she can.
Should this work please, a larger one I plan,
Fully adorned through many pages' span.

J. V. D. V.

EMANVRIES E IOANVRE D (oval border text)

ÆTAT.77.

Cum privil.

Sim. Gondius fecit.

Ipse ego, qui primis *Artem veneratus ab annis*,
    Hoc studui, vt nullum tempus abiret iners.
Grata oculis animóque fuit dîa Optica *nostris*,
    Atque animo accessit qui facit esse, labor,
Hanc etenim per lustra octo studiosius artem
    Excolui. studio, quod doceo, obtinui.
Dicitur ars certa hæc pariat quam regula certa:
    Traditur hîc certis Optica *docta modis.*
Ars regit hæc oculos, animos recreátque videndo:
    Non oculos falsis ludit imaginibus.
Exaĉté sculptis ars hîc proposta figuris,
    Vt vestris oculis gratius esset opus.
Fórté aliquod nomen mihi erit: sed Belgica *docta,*
    Si quod nomen erit, quærat & ipsa sibi.
Hæc si grata oculis; occurret maior imago:
    Hanc exornatam pagina multa dabit.

                  I.V.F.

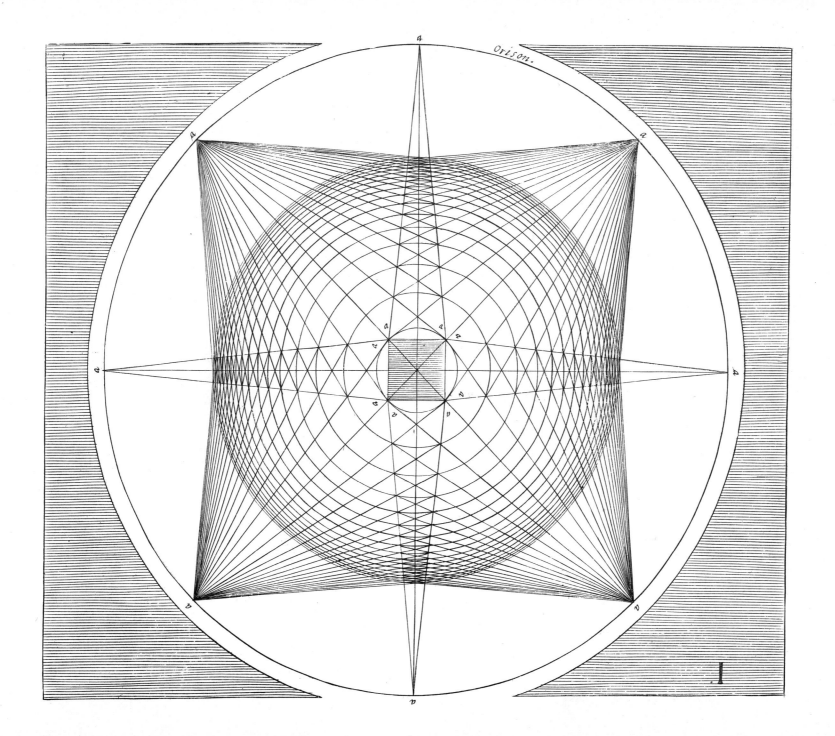

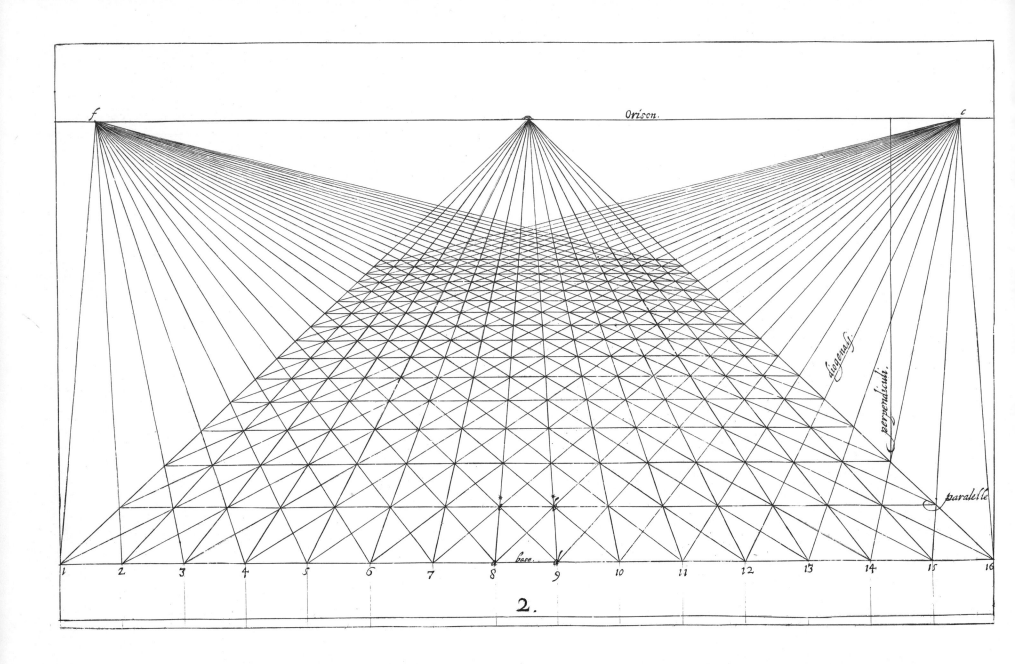

Orison.

Diagonal.

perpendicular.

paralelle

base.

f   c

1   2   3   4   5   6   7   8   9   10   11   12   13   14   15   16

2.

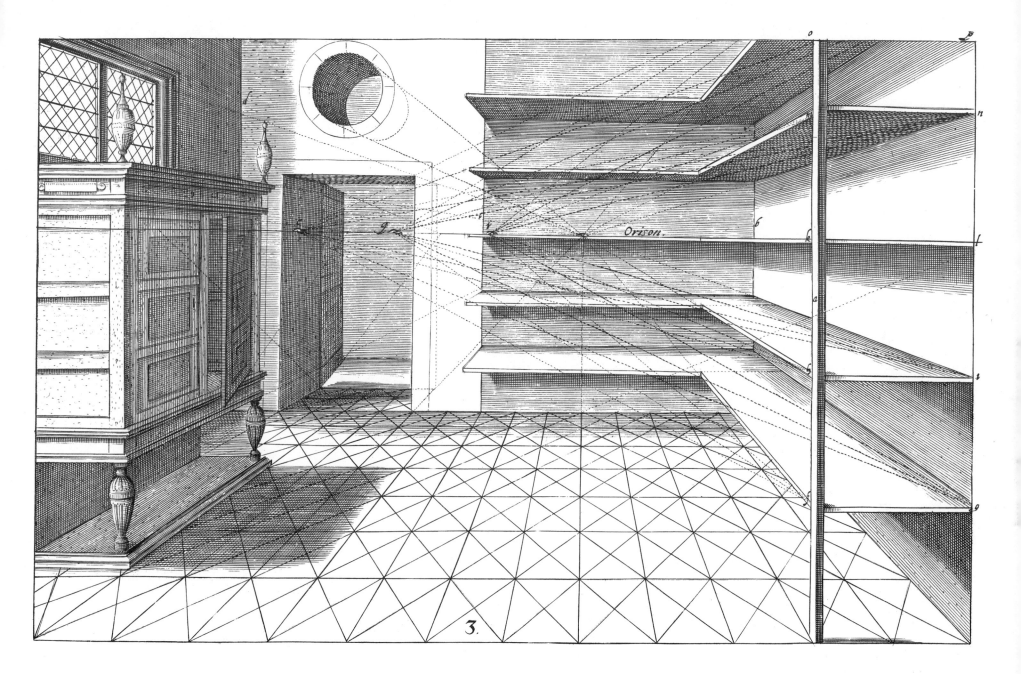

Orison.

3.

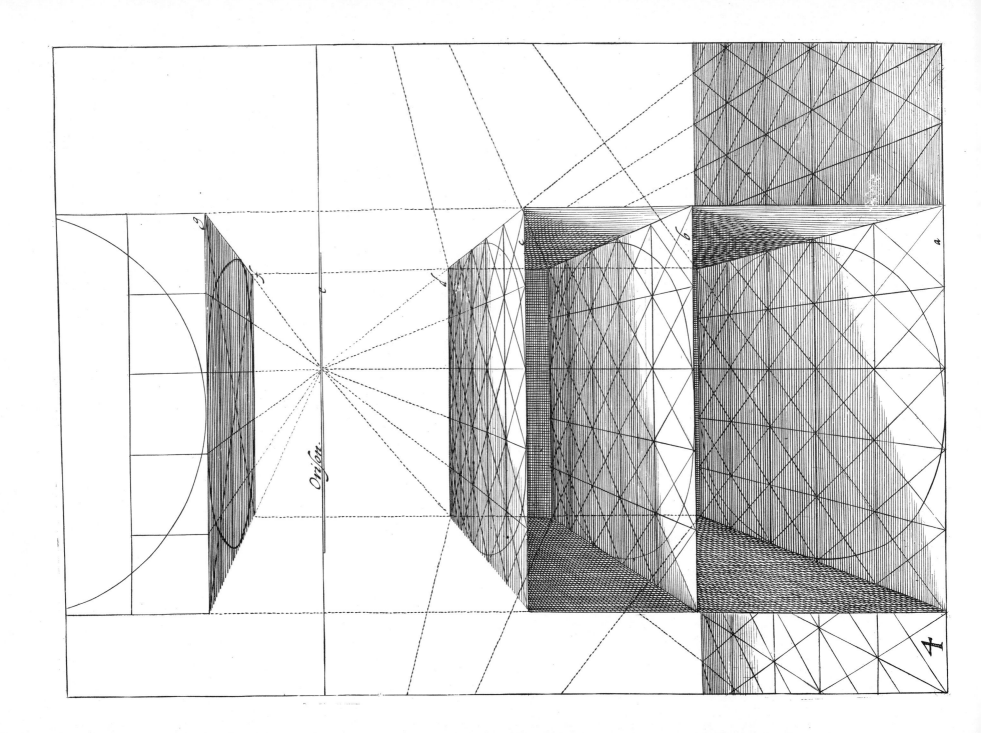

Orizon.

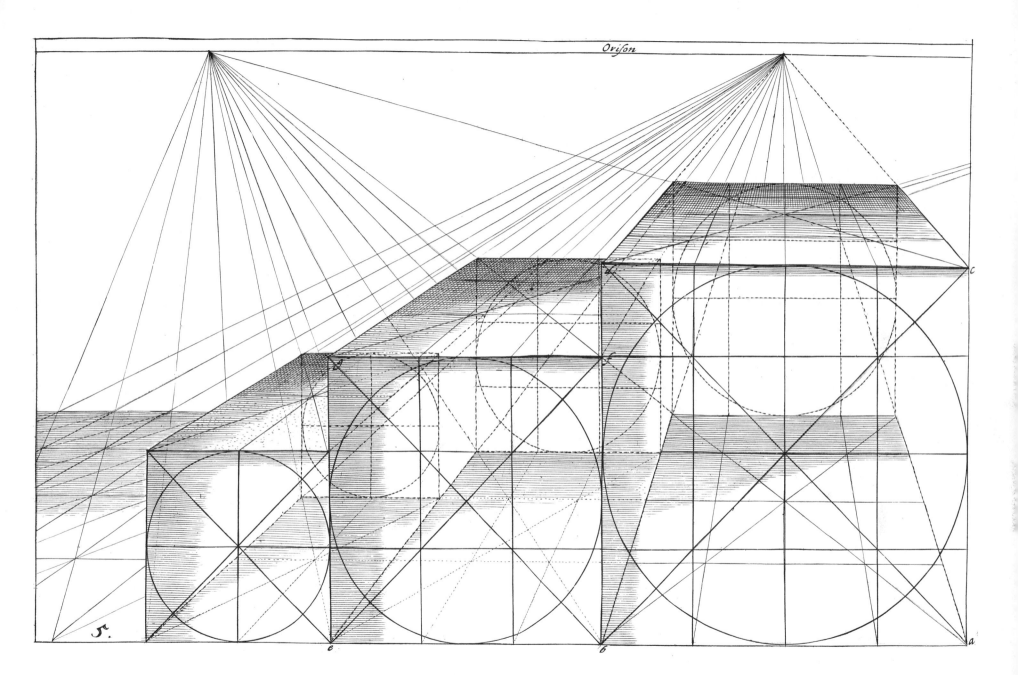

Orifon

5.

e

b

a

c

Orison

7.

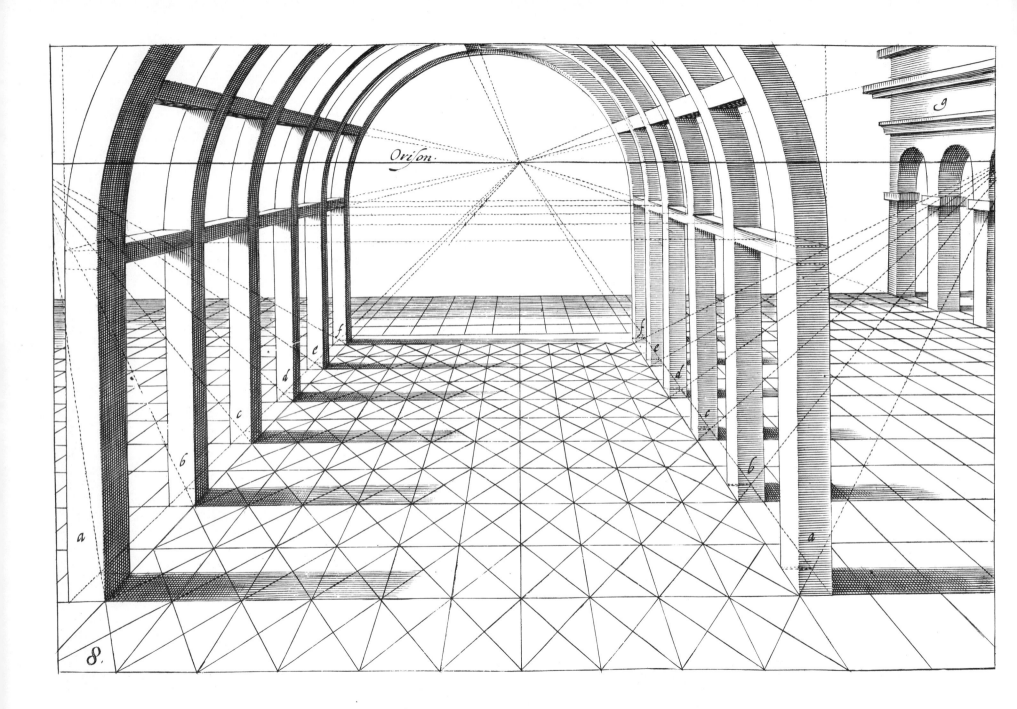

Orifon.

8.

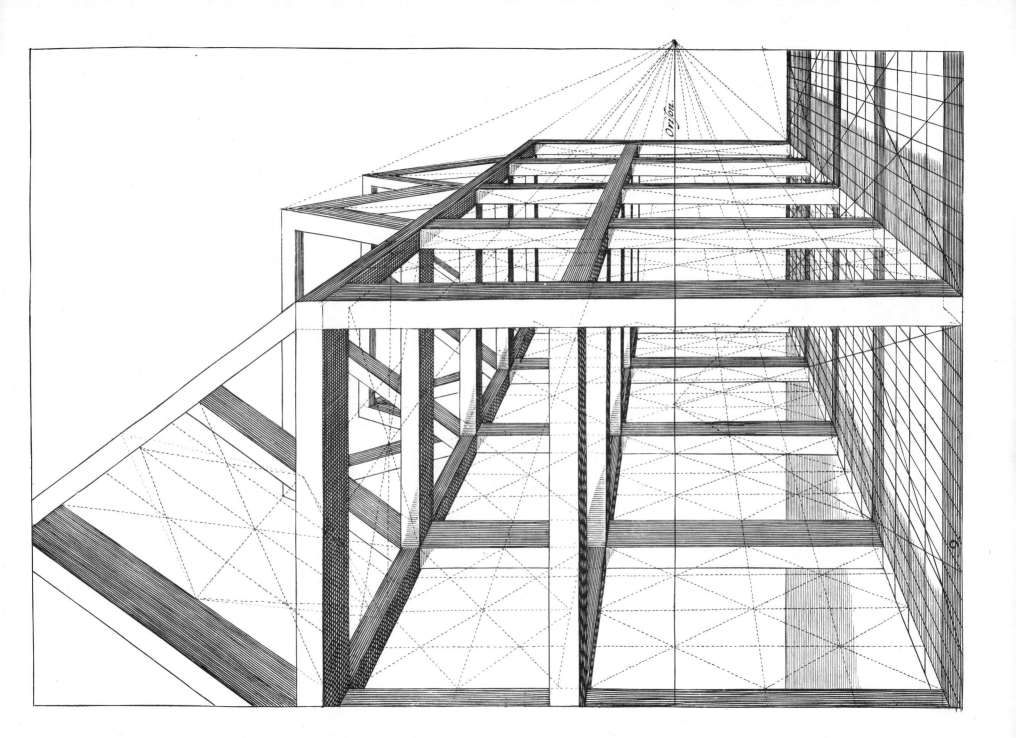

Orison

1604

5

II.

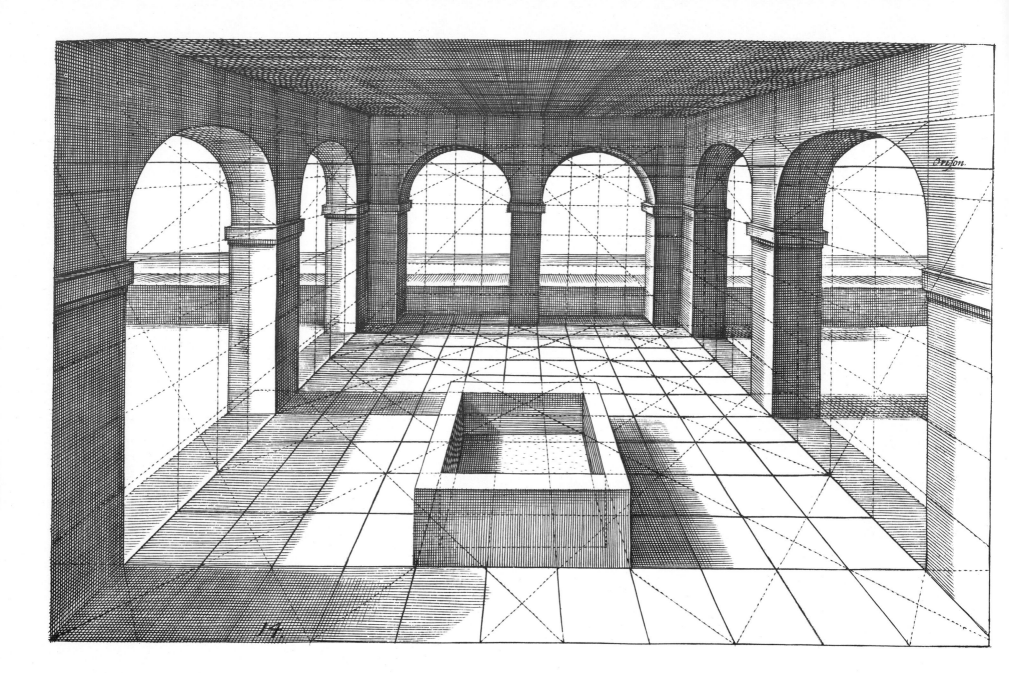

Orison.

1604

Orison

15.

Orison.

Orison

18

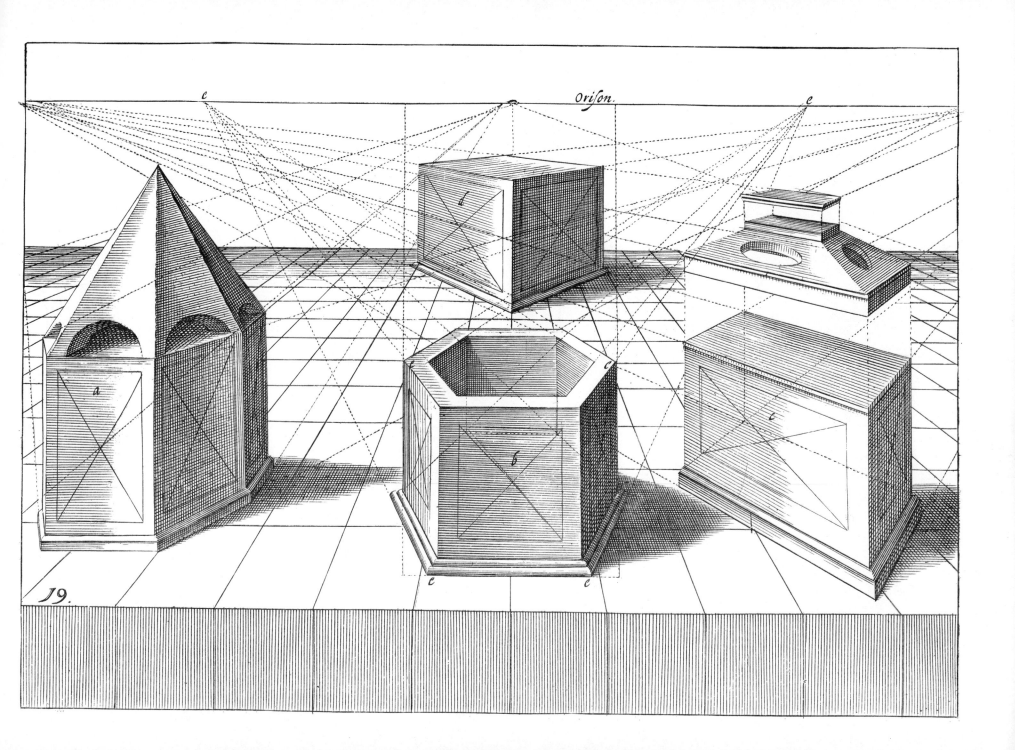

orison

19.

Orison.

21

Orison.

22.

Orisoni

24.

Hh. exc.
1604.

ogson.

d

c

b

a

e

f

25

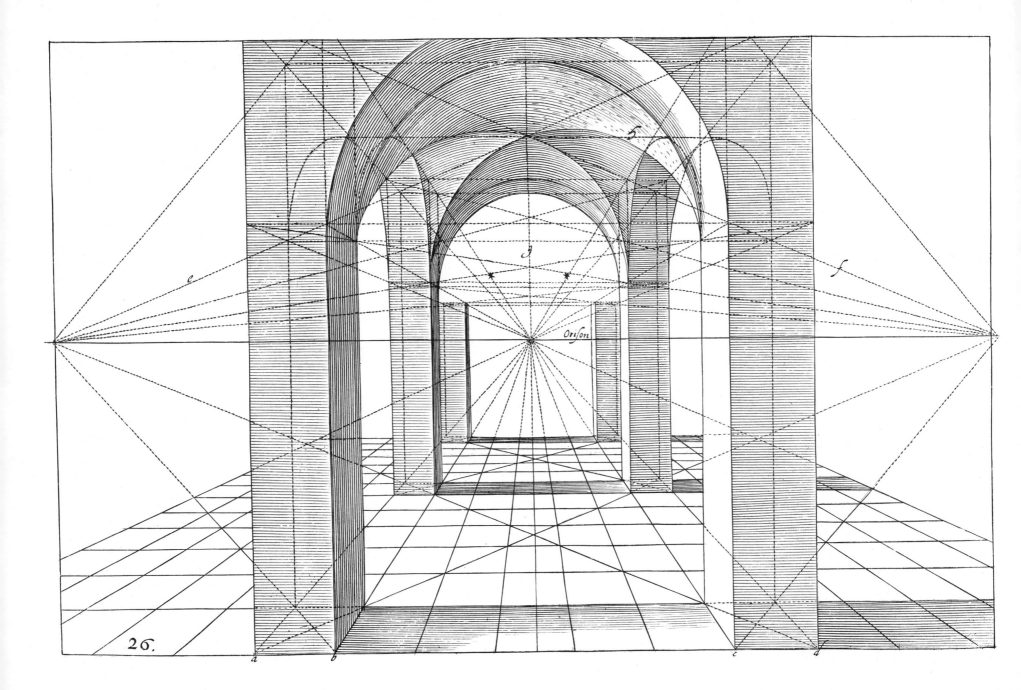

Orison

27.

Orison.

28.

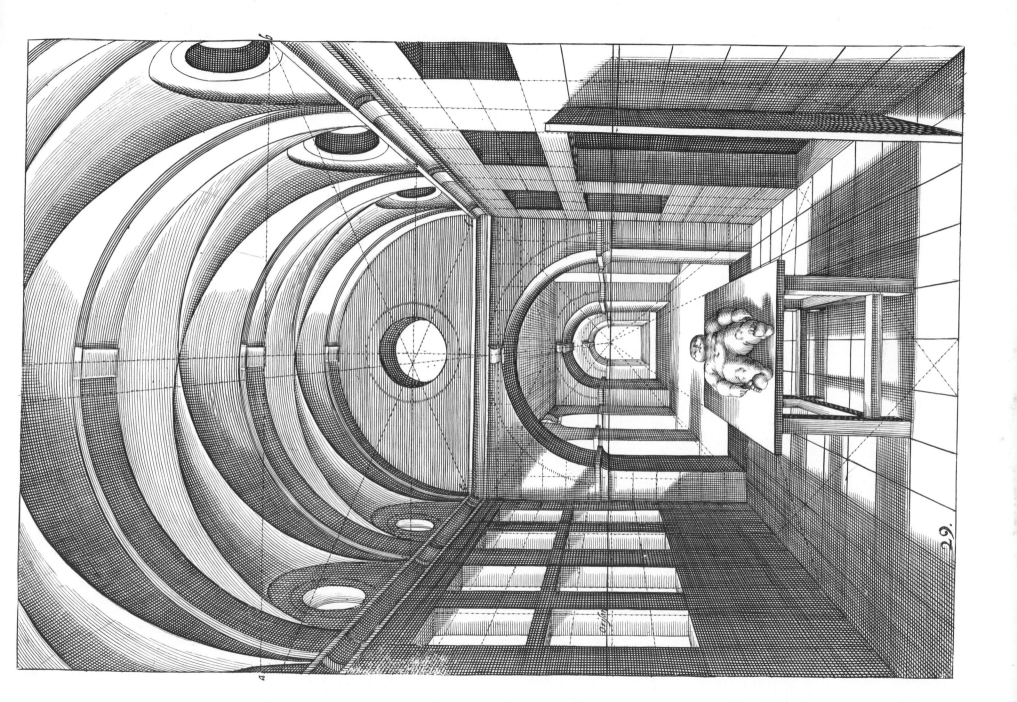

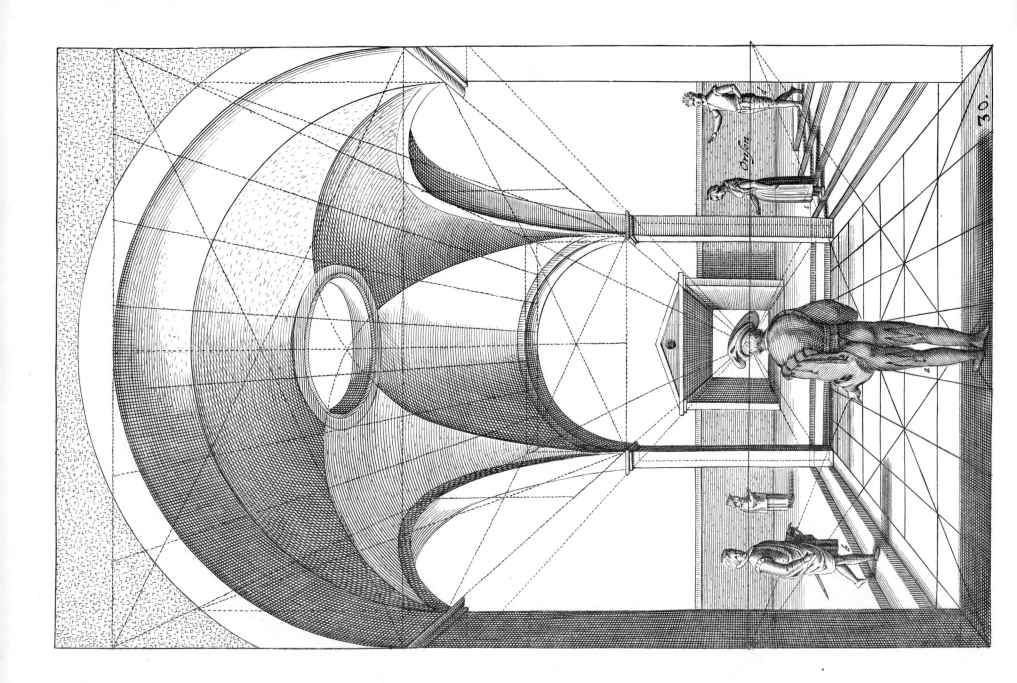

Orylon

32.

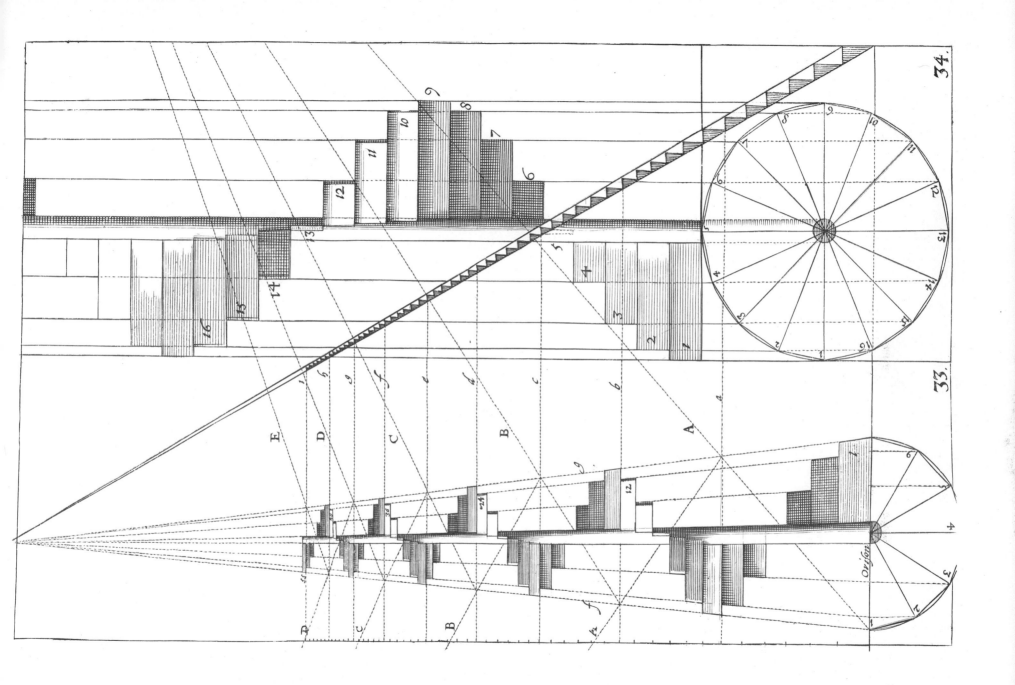

Orison

vriese Inv.

36

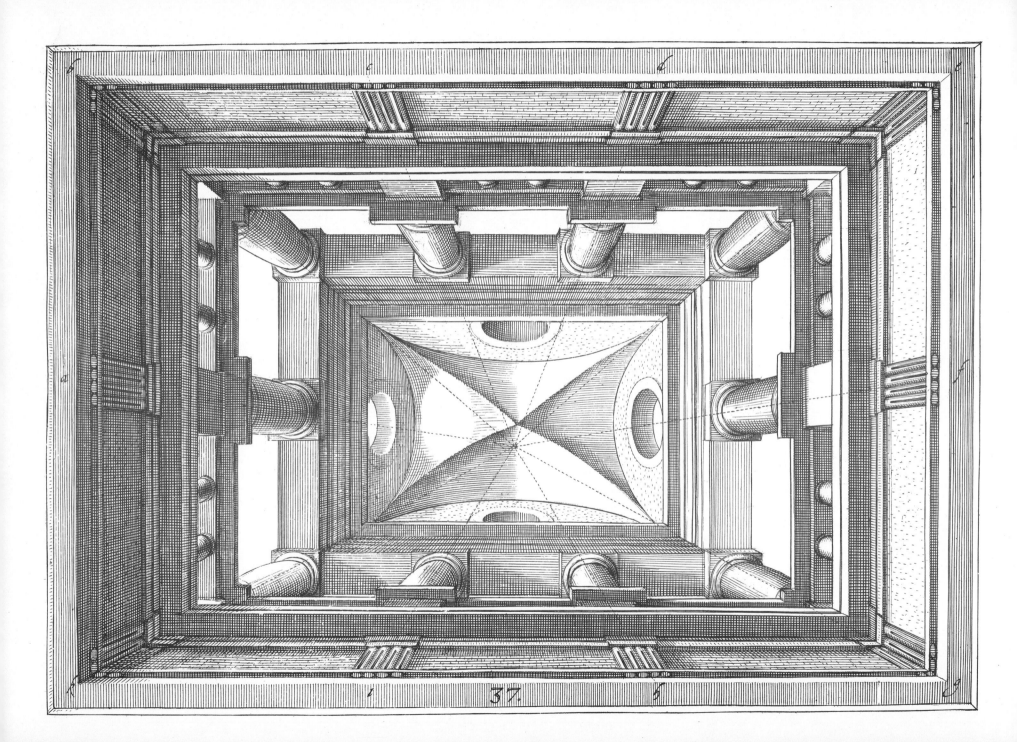

37.

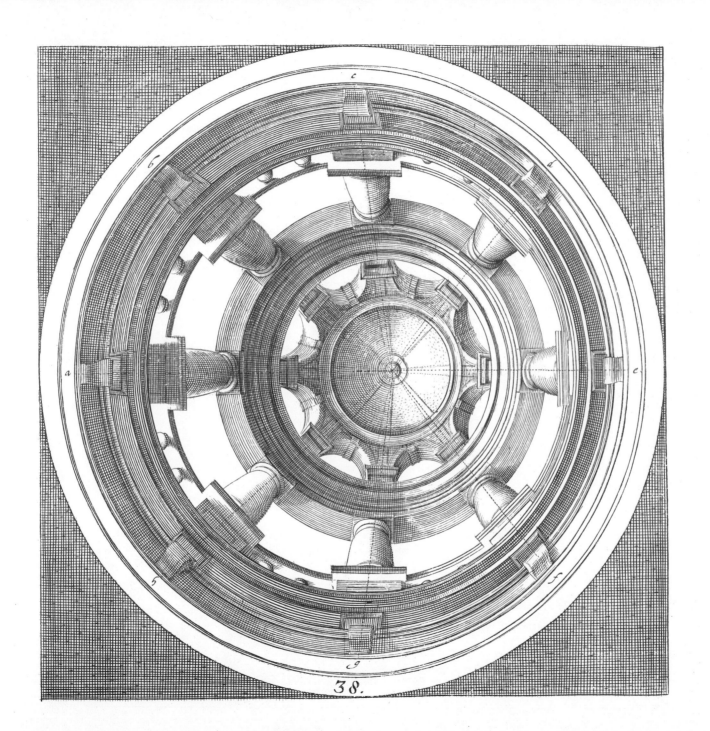

38.

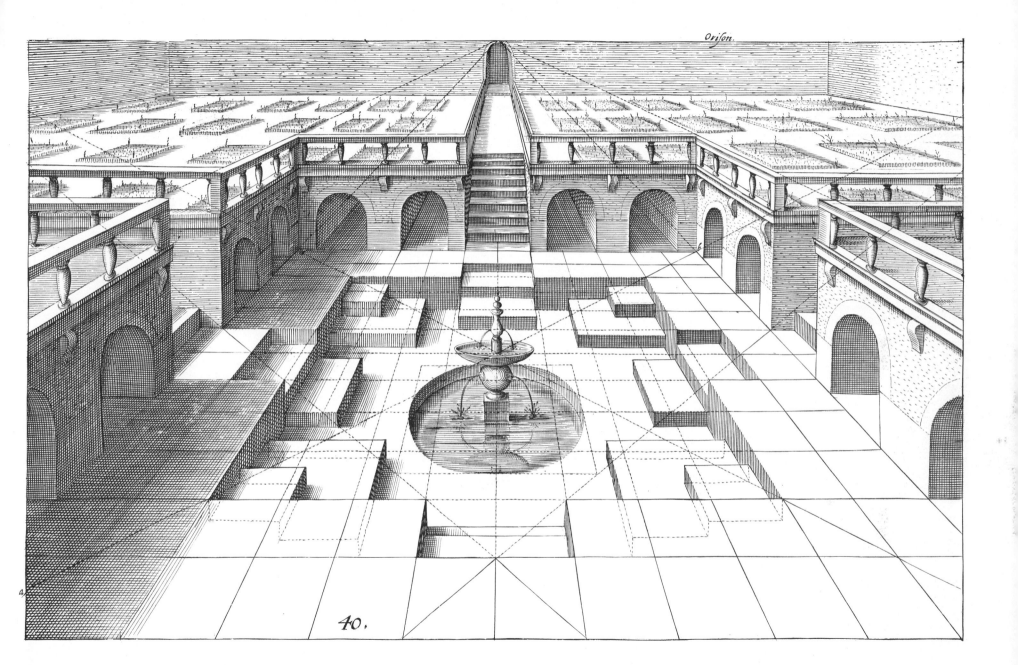

40.

Orfeu.

42

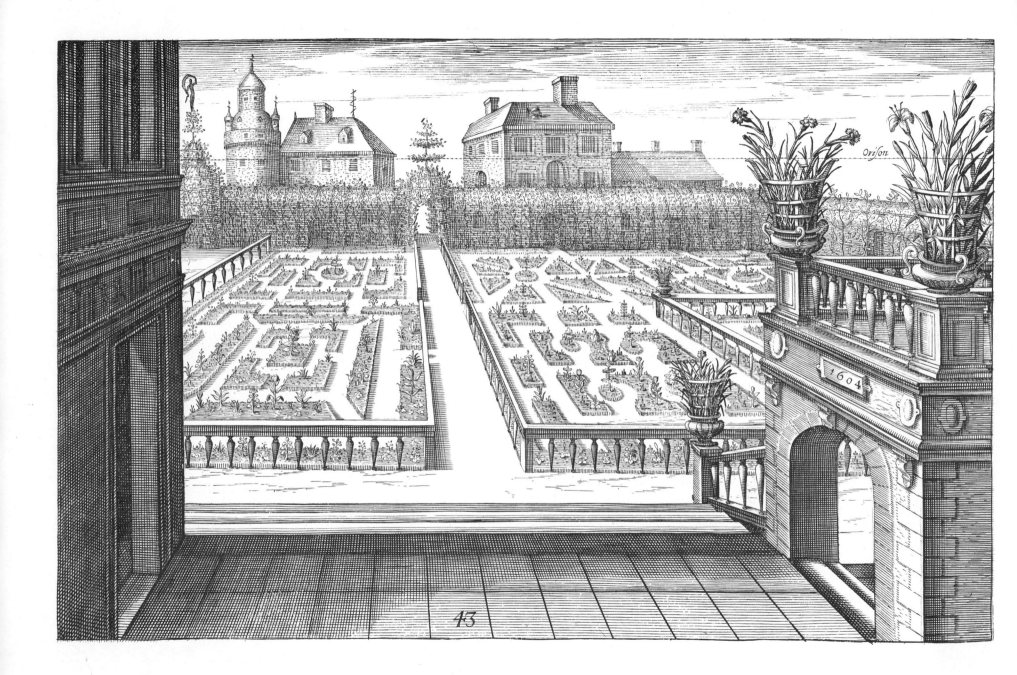

Orison

1604

43

Orise   Occident

Oriov.

Anno,   1604

46.

7.

8.

9.

Orison.

1604

48.

Tuscbana. 1.

Dorica. 2.

Ionica. 3.

10.

Hh
Sculp
sit.
et
exc.

An
no
1604

Orison.

Corinthia. 4.

49.

11

11
10
9
8
7
6
5
4
3
2
1

Composita. 5

PERSPECTIVE

PARS ALTERA,
IN QVA

Præstantissima quæque Artis præcepta, nec non eximia ac scitu digniora argumenta circa magnifica aliquot AEdificia & præclara Architecturæ decora plenè planèque exhibentur, addita brevi sed dilucida Linearum ac Fundamentorum descriptione.

In gratiam Ingeniosorum Studiosorúmque hominum publicata.

Auctore Iohanne Vredemanno Frisio.

HENRIC. HONDIVS SCVLPS.
ET EXCVD. CVM PRIVILL.

LVGDVNI   BATAVORVM.

Translation of Latin title page to Part Two (preceding page):

PERSPECTIVE
SECOND PART

IN WHICH

All the most outstanding precepts of the Art, as well as excellent and noteworthy discussions of several magnificent Buildings and celebrated ornaments of Architecture, are fully and clearly set forth, with the addition of a brief but lucid description of lines and bases.
Published for the gratification of talented and studious men.

By Jan Vredeman de Vries.

ENGRAVED AND LEGALLY PUBLISHED BY
HENRICUS HONDIUS
LEIDEN

Orison

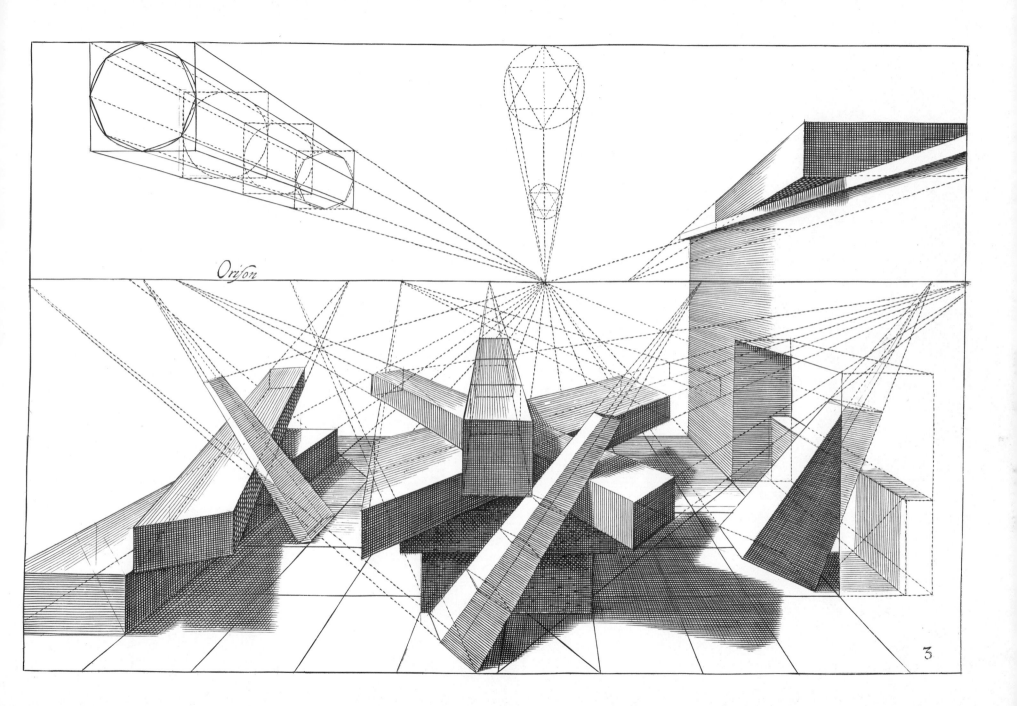

Orison

3

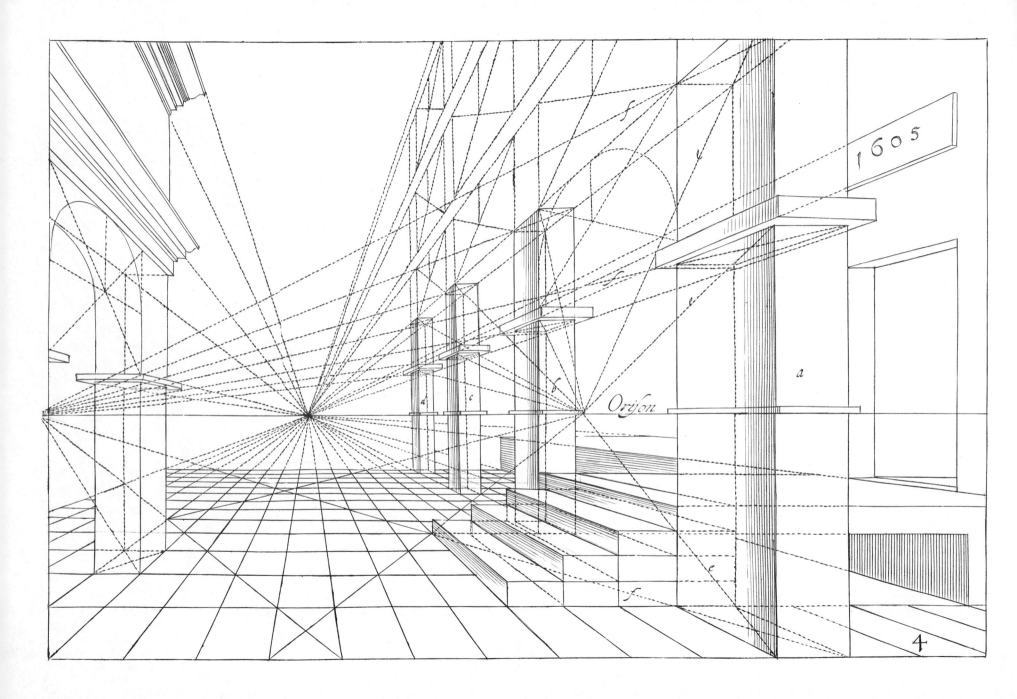

Orifon

1605

4

Orison.

Orison

7

Orison

12

13

P. V. *inv.*   *Hondius Sculp.*

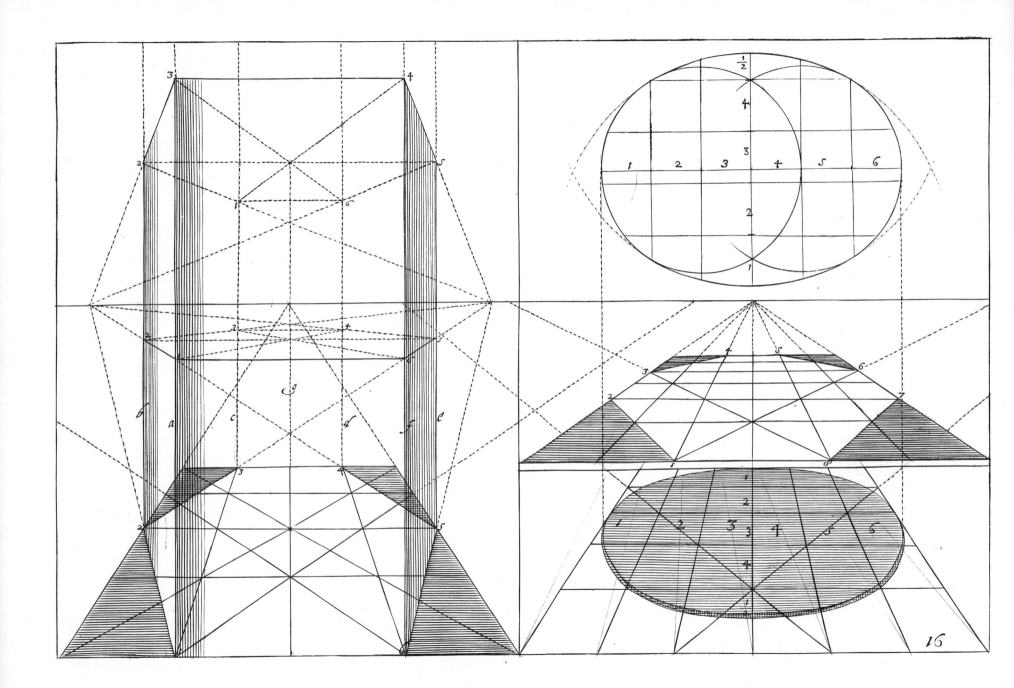

16

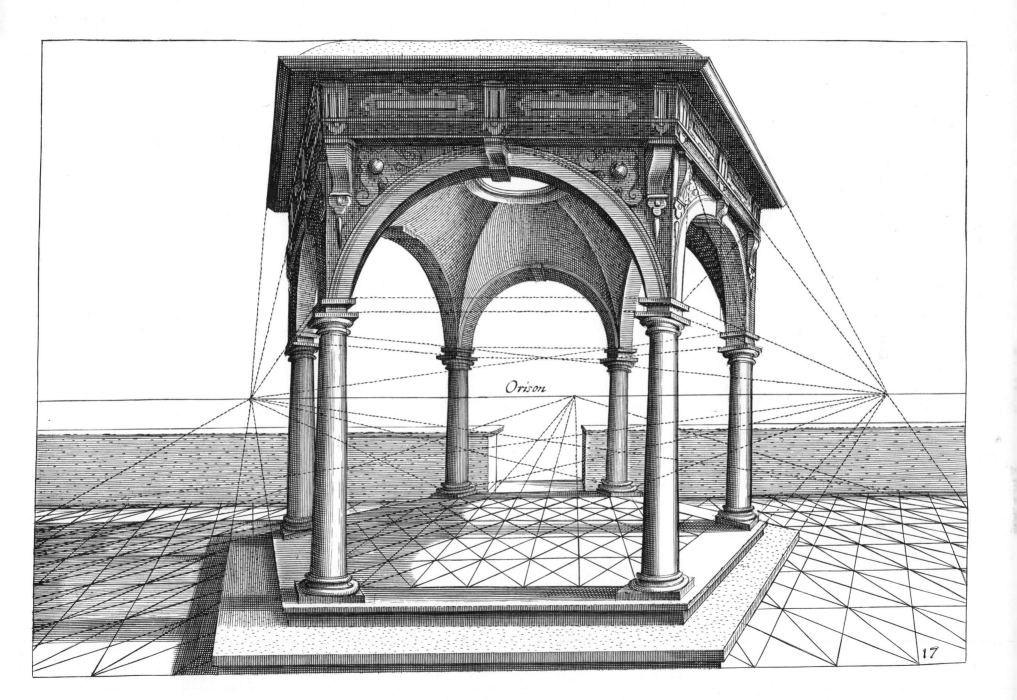

Orison

17

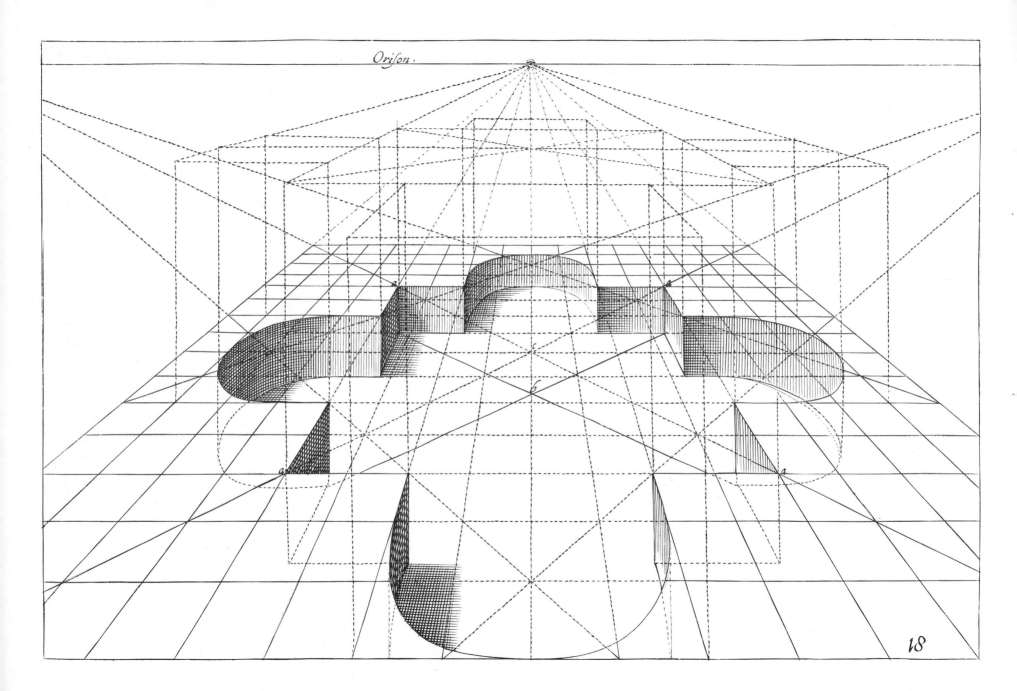

Orison.

18

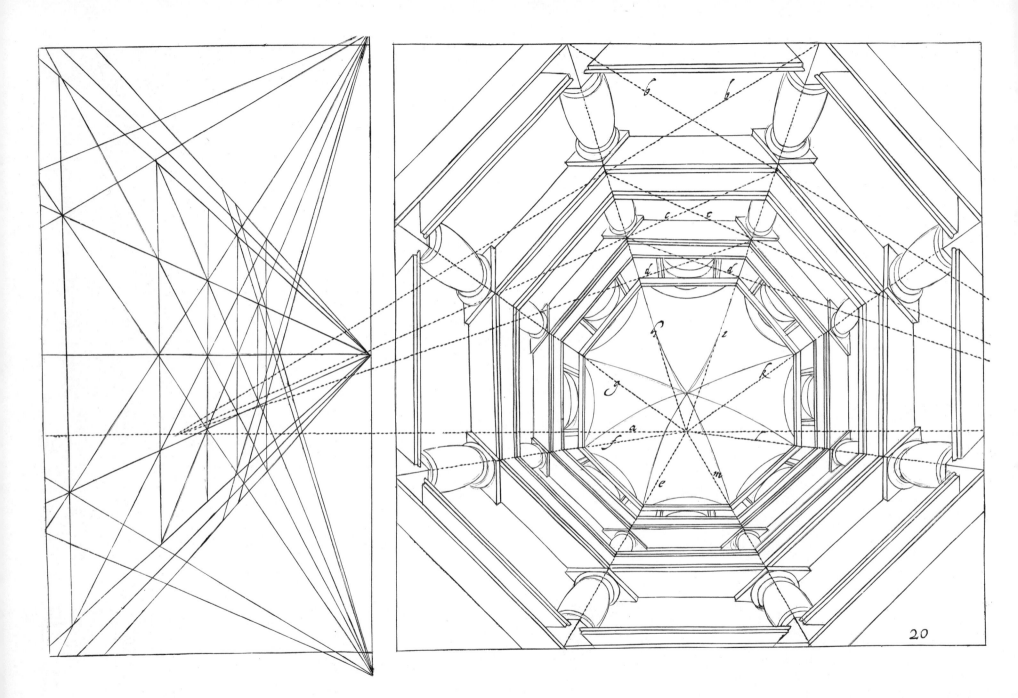

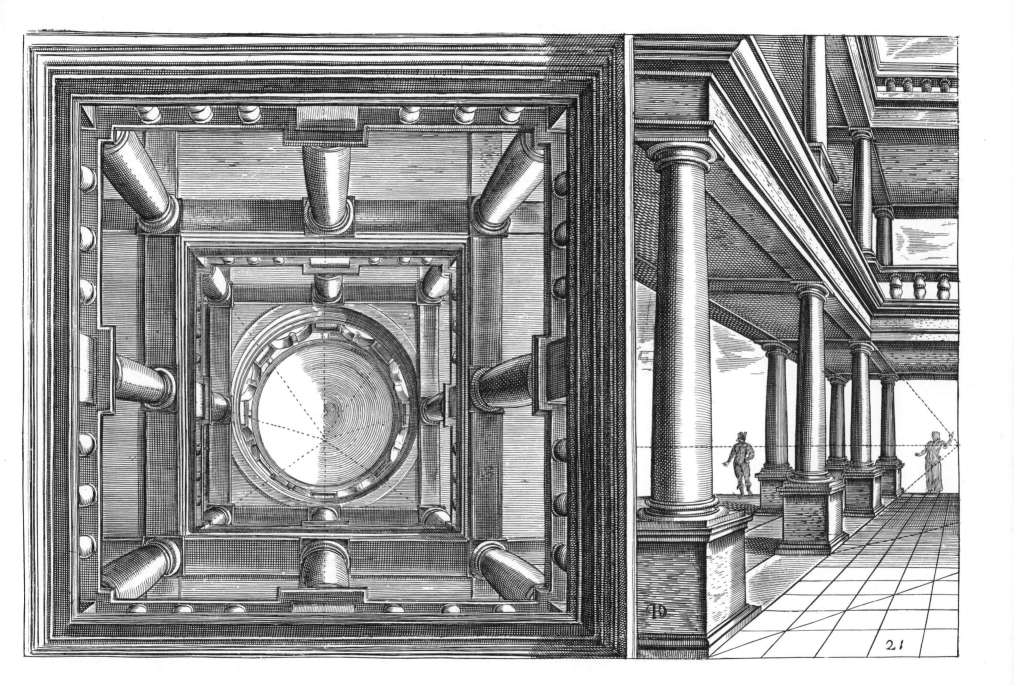

21

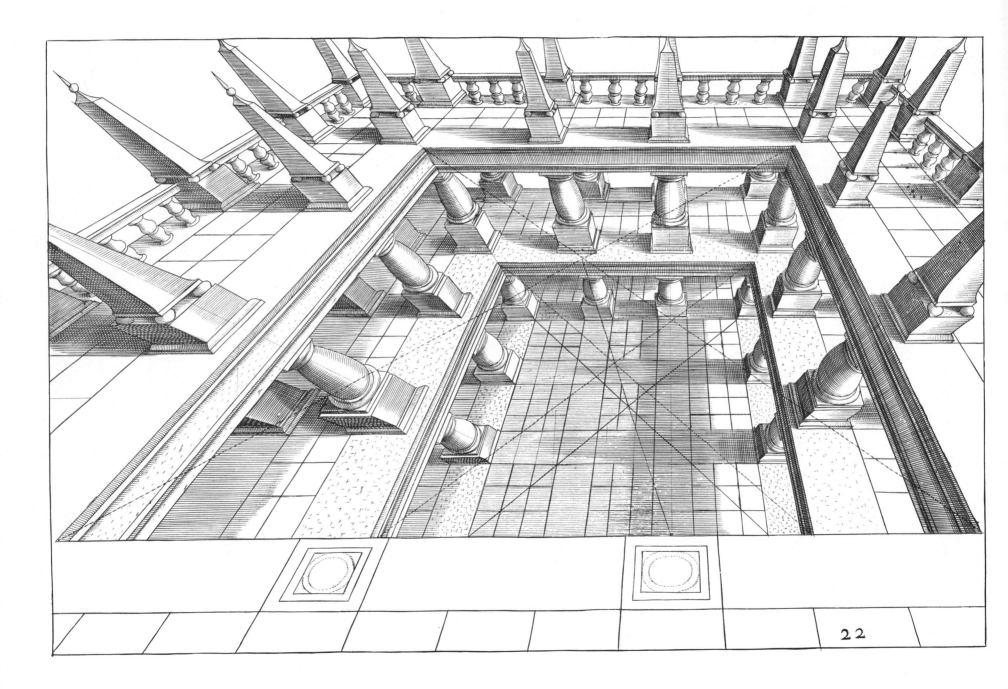

22

VRIES. INVENT. 1608

23

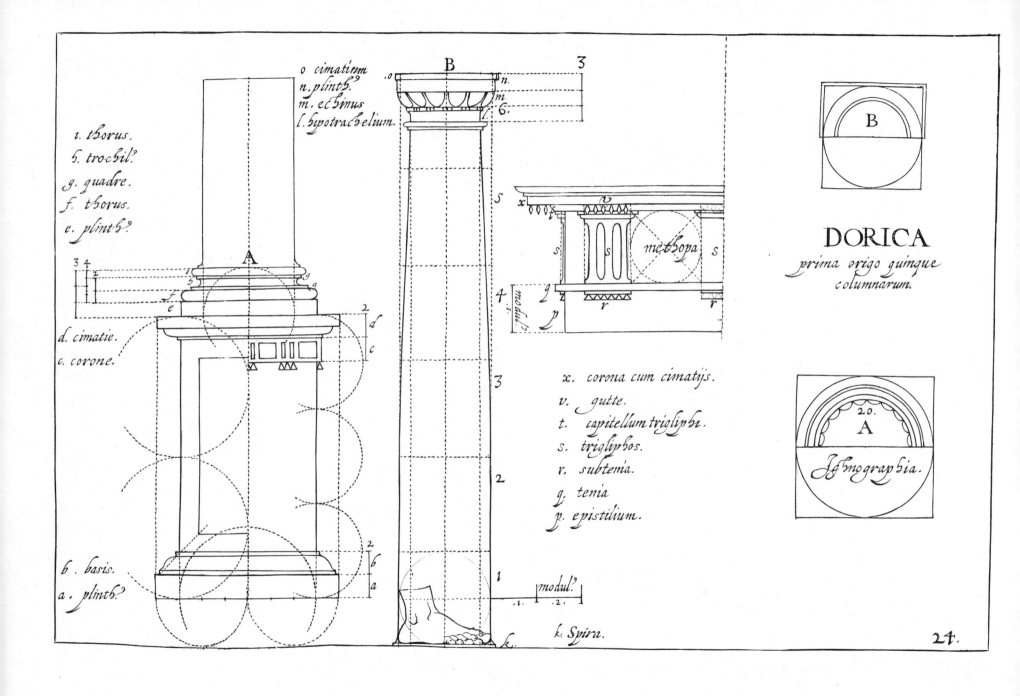

o cimatium
n. plinth?
m. echinus
l. hypotrachelium.

1. thorus.
h. trochil?
g. quadre.
f. thorus.
e. plinth?

d. cimatie.
c. corone.

b. basis.
a. plinth?

metopa

DORICA
prima origo quinque
columnarum.

x. corona cum cimatijs.
v. gutte.
t. capitellum triglyphi.
s. triglyphos.
r. subtenia.
q. tenia
p. epistilium.

k. Spira.

modul?

Ichnographia.

24.